The U.S. Armed Forces

The U.S. Marine Corps

by Matt Doeden

Consultant:
Barbara J. Fox
Reading Specialist
North Carolina State University

Capstone
press

Mankato, Minnesota

Blazers is published by Capstone Press
151 Good Counsel Drive, P.O. Box 669, Mankato, Minnesota 56002
www.capstonepress.com

Library of Congress Cataloging-in-Publication Data
Doeden, Matt.
    The U.S. Marine Corps / by Matt Doeden.
    p. cm.—(Blazers. The U.S. Armed Forces)
    Includes bibliographical references and index.
    Contents: The U.S. Marine Corps in action—Marine vehicles—Weapons
and equipment—Marine jobs.
    ISBN 0-7368-2739-0 (hardcover)
    1. United States. Marine Corps—Juvenile literature. [1. United States.
Marine Corps.] I. Title.
VE23.D64 2005
359.9′6′0973—dc22   2003024376

Editorial Credits
Carrie A. Braulick, editor; Juliette Peters, designer; Jo Miller, photo researcher;
    Eric Kudalis, product planning editor

Photo Credits
Capstone Press/Gary Sundermeyer, cover (inset)
Corbis/Aero Graphics Inc, 22; AFP Earnie Grafton, 20
DoD photo by CPO Alan Baribeau, USN, 5; LCpl S. A. Harwood, USMC, 21
    (top), 23
DVIC/PHCM Terry Mitchell, USN, 6–7
Fotodynamics/Ted Carlson, 12, 13, 15, 25, 28–29
Getty Images Inc./Gabriel Mistral, 21 (bottom); Joe Raedle, 9; Robert Nickelsberg,
    27; Scott Nelson, 16–17; Scott Olson, 26; Sean Smith, 14
U.S. Marine Corps photo by Sgt. Kevin R. Reed, 19
U.S. Navy Photo by PH1 Richard Rosser, 11; PH2 Michael Sandberg, 8; PHAR
    Staci Bitzer, cover

**Capstone Press thanks Major Daryl G. Crane, Executive Officer, Assault Amphibian
School, U.S. Marine Corps Base Camp Pendleton, California, for his assistance in
preparing this book.**

1 2 3 4 5 6 09 08 07 06 05 04

Table of Contents

The U.S. Marine Corps in Action

Sixteen Marines sit in an AAV. The AAV quietly moves through the ocean. More AAVs follow closely behind.

Assault Amphibian Vehicles (AAVs)

★ ★ ★ ★ ★ ★ ★ ★ ★ ★ ★ ★

The AAVs reach the shore near an enemy base. Enemy troops shoot at them. Thick armor on the AAVs protects the Marines inside.

The U.S. government formed the Marine Corps to protect U.S. ships from pirates.

The Marines open doors at the rear of the vehicles. They rush into the enemy base. The Marines capture the enemy crew. Their mission is a success.

Marine Vehicles

Marine pilots fly AV-8B
Harrier jets. Harriers can
hover like helicopters.

The AH-1W Super Cobra helicopter attacks targets on the ground. Marines use it to protect troops.

Abrams tanks

AAV

Thick metal armor protects tanks and AAVs. Abrams tanks fight enemy ground forces. AAVs carry Marines in water and over land.

AV-8B Harrier Diagram

Cockpit

Bomb

Wing

Fuel tank

Missile

17

Weapons and Equipment

Marines have powerful weapons. The lightweight M-16 rifle quickly fires bullets.

Squad automatic weapon

Marines use weapons to destroy targets. Cannons called howitzers shoot explosive shells. Some weapons fire powerful rockets.

Howitzer

BLAZER FACT

The M-198 Howitzer can be dropped by a parachute onto a battlefield.

Rocket launcher

Night-vision goggles

Marines use binoculars
and night-vision goggles to
help them see. They talk
to each other with radios.

Marine Jobs

Marines have different jobs. Many Marines perform combat duties. Others are pilots or mechanics.

Marines can be enlisted members or officers. Officers have a higher rank than enlisted members. All marines are ready for missions on short notice.

MARINE CORPS RANKS

★ ★ ★ ★ ★ ★ ★ ★ ★ ★ ★ ★ ★ ★ ★ ★ ★

ENLISTED	OFFICERS
Private	Lieutenant
Corporal	Captain
Sergeant	Major
Staff Sergeant	Colonel
Gunnery Sergeant	General
Master Sergeant	
Master Gunnery Sergeant	

BLAZER FACT

The Marines are called America's 911 force because they quickly respond to emergencies.

Harriers

Glossary

armor (AR-mur)—a protective metal covering

cannon (KAN-uhn)—a large gun that fires shells

combat (KOM-bat)—fighting between military forces

howitzer (HOU-uht-sur)—a cannon that shoots explosive shells long distances

mechanic (muh-KAN-ik)—a person who fixes machinery

mission (MISH-uhn)—a military task

rank (RANGK)—an official position or job level

shell (SHEL)—a large bullet fired from a cannon

Read More

Abramovitz, Melissa. *The U.S. Marine Corps at War.* On the Front Lines. Mankato, Minn.: Capstone Press, 2002.

Cooper, Jason. *U.S. Marine Corps.* Fighting Forces. Vero Beach, Fla.: Rourke, 2004.

Green, Michael, and Gladys Green. *Assault Amphibian Vehicles: The AAVs.* War Machines. Mankato, Minn.: Edge Books, 2004.

Internet Sites

FactHound offers a safe, fun way to find Internet sites related to this book. All of the sites on FactHound have been researched by our staff.

Here's how:

1. Visit *www.facthound.com*
2. Type in this special code **0736827390** for age-appropriate sites. Or enter a search word related to this book for a more general search.
3. Click on the **Fetch It** button.

FactHound will fetch the best sites for you!

Index